Date: 4/21/21

**J 613.69 HAY
Hayes, Vicki C.,
Surviving a blizzard /**

SURVIVAL STORIES

SURVIVING A
BLIZZARD

By Vicki C. Hayes

WORLD BOOK

The Quest for Discovery Never Ends

This edition is co-published by agreement between Kaleidoscope and World Book, Inc.

Kaleidoscope Publishing, Inc.
6012 Blue Circle Drive
Minnetonka, MN 55343 U.S.A.

World Book, Inc.
180 North LaSalle St., Suite 900
Chicago IL 60601 U.S.A.

Kaleidoscope ISBNs
978-1-64519-200-8 (library bound)
978-1-64519-268-8 (ebook)

World Book ISBN
978-0-7166-4168-1 (library bound)

Library of Congress Control Number
2020935890

Developed and produced by Focus Strategic Communications Inc.

Printed in the United States of America.

FIND ME IF YOU CAN!

Bigfoot lurks within one of the images in this book. It's up to you to find him!

TABLE OF
CONTENTS

Stranded in a Car

Jim and Jennifer Stolpa held their baby close. Clayton was only four months old. They had to keep him warm. They huddled together in their snowbound car. Outside a **blizzard** was howling. They had been driving to Idaho, but when the snowstorm got worse, the main highway was closed.

Jim had decided to take a shortcut. It was an unlucky decision. Their car got stuck 150 miles (240 km) from the nearest town. No one knew where they were. No one would rescue them.

Getting stuck in a car in a snowstorm can be very dangerous, especially in remote areas.

Blizzards can make driving almost impossible.

Jennifer and her baby took shelter in a cave. Jim continued to search for help.

It was New Year's Day in 1993. They had been trapped for four days and nights. Their food was running low. Jim and Jennifer decided to take their chances out in the storm. They gathered leftover food and a sleeping bag. They climbed out into the blizzard.

For 12 hours, they trudged through knee-deep snow. When night came, they had to stop because they were too tired and cold to keep walking.

They found a hollow under a snow-covered bush. Jennifer and the baby huddled in the sleeping bag. Coyotes howled nearby. Temperatures dropped below zero (-18°C).

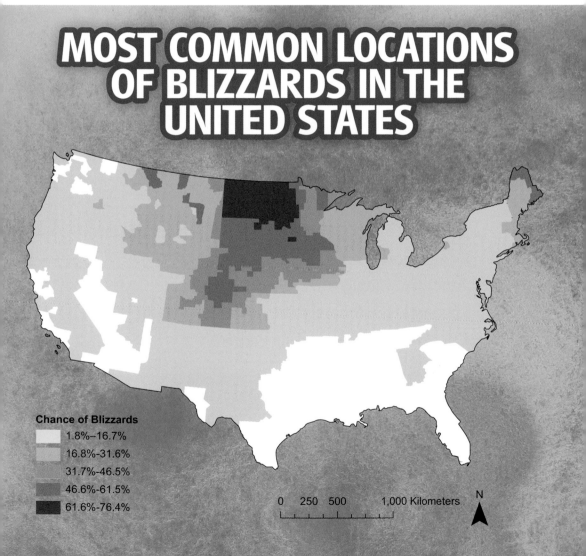

MOST COMMON LOCATIONS OF BLIZZARDS IN THE UNITED STATES

Chance of Blizzards
- 1.8%–16.7%
- 16.8%-31.6%
- 31.7%-46.5%
- 46.6%-61.5%
- 61.6%-76.4%

0   250   500   1,000 Kilometers

N

Dusty Ferguson searched through the snow to find the Stolpas.

Jim kept walking. He trudged for 30 miles (50 km) in driving snow. He had terrible frostbite and hypothermia. Finally, he came to a house. He was so frozen he could barely talk, but he was able to describe where he had left his family.

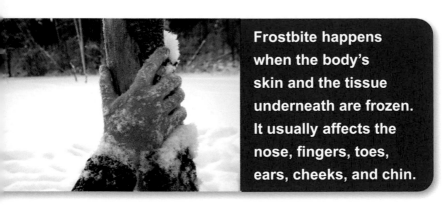

Frostbite happens when the body's skin and the tissue underneath are frozen. It usually affects the nose, fingers, toes, ears, cheeks, and chin.

Rescue crews went out. After two days in the snow cave, Jennifer and Clayton were found. They had survived. The family was reunited in the hospital. Jim and Jennifer lost toes to frostbite. Baby Clayton was fine.

FUN FACT

In 1994, a TV movie called *Snowbound* was made about the Stolpa family's survival. It starred Neil Patrick Harris and was shown on CBS.

Hypothermia occurs when the body's temperature drops dangerously low. Hypothermia can make it hard to think clearly or move well.

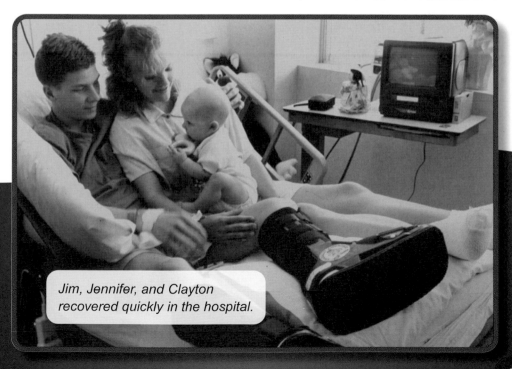

Jim, Jennifer, and Clayton recovered quickly in the hospital.

Stuck on the Mountain

Yevgeniy Krasnitskiy and his three friends grabbed onto their tents. The snowstorm was fierce. They were trapped on Mount Rainier. Yev, Rus, Vasily, and Constantine had been working their way to the summit at 14,410 feet (4,392 m).

At 13,500 feet (4,115 m), Rus got mountain sickness, so the friends set up camp. Then, the evening storm came. High winds ripped through their gear. Much of it was blown down the steep, icy slopes.

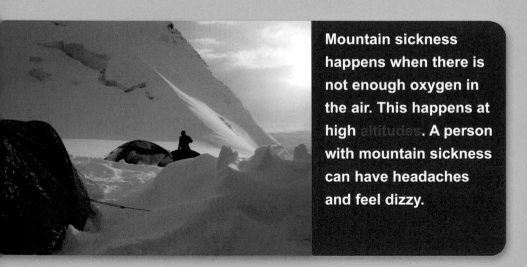

Mountain sickness happens when there is not enough oxygen in the air. This happens at high altitudes. A person with mountain sickness can have headaches and feel dizzy.

FUN FACT

The Native American name for Mount Rainier is *Tacoma*. It means "mother of waters" and "great white mountain."

First thing the next morning, the friends called 911. Ten minutes later, a helicopter appeared. But the wind was gusting at 50 miles an hour (80 kph). The helicopter could not land. The next morning, a bigger military helicopter came. It could not land either.

The friends spent a third night in the wind and snow. They huddled together inside their one

Helicopters are common in mountain rescues.

remaining tent. During the night, rocks and ice slid down the mountain and smashed into the tent. Luckily, the friends had slept with their helmets on.

Mountain climbers must be careful not to get caught in a blizzard or avalanche.

By now, the friends were weak and exhausted. Their feet were numb and blue. Their supplies were almost gone. They kept hearing helicopters, but none could land. They knew they had to move. It was too risky to go down the mountain. They decided to go up and over it instead.

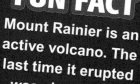

FUN FACT

Mount Rainier is an active volcano. The last time it erupted was about 1,000 years ago.

At dusk, they got to within 400 feet (120 m) of the summit. They spent the night in an ice cave as shelter from the wind and snow. They crowded into two sleeping bags. Then on Thursday morning, they made it to the summit. For a very short time, the winds stopped. Quickly, a helicopter landed. After being stranded for four days, the friends were finally rescued.

Helicopters have trouble landing when the pilot cannot see clearly.

Frozen at the Bottom of the World

In 1914, Ernest Shackleton and his crew of 28 men watched the *Endurance* get trapped and crushed by ice. Their ship had pushed through the icy seas toward **Antarctica** for more than 1,000 miles (1,600 km). Then, a big freeze came.

For two days, the men climbed out on the ice and tried to chop the ship free. At night, they listened to the **hull** crack as the sea refroze. The men unloaded the ship. They waited helplessly on the floating ice pack for 281 days. They watched their ship splinter. Then, it disappeared into the ice.

FUN FACT

There were 70 sled dogs and a male cat named Mrs. Chippy on the *Endurance*.

Ernest and his crew tried digging *the* Endurance *out of the ice.*

Eventually, the Endurance *sank below the ice.*

Ernest had wanted to walk across Antarctica. Now, he and his crew were hundreds of miles from land with no ship. They started walking on the ice. They dragged three lifeboats behind them. After 346 miles (557 km), they got to open water.

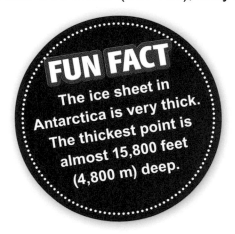

FUN FACT

The ice sheet in Antarctica is very thick. The thickest point is almost 15,800 feet (4,800 m) deep.

Ernest directs his crew as they pull the lifeboats across the ice.

Elephant Island is off the coast of Antarctica.

FUN FACT

Today, Elephant Island is home to a research center named Goeldi. Up to six researchers can stay for no more than 40 days during the summer.

They sailed to Elephant Island. But no one knew where they were. Ernest needed to get to South Georgia Island. It was 800 miles (1,300 km) away. He took five men on one lifeboat. The remaining 22 crew members stayed behind.

The seas were wild. The boat was drenched with massive waves and freezing spray. The deck was covered with ice. After 14 days, the men made it to South Georgia Island.

Ernest and two men hiked 22 miles (35 km) across a huge mountain range. They crossed **glaciers**, icy slopes, and snow fields. They lowered themselves down a 30-foot (9-m) waterfall between ice cliffs. They made it to a **whaling station**.

Ernest took a whaling boat to get the three men he had left on the other side of the mountain. Then, he had to save the men on Elephant Island. The sea was still full of pack ice. It took three months before the 22 men were safely rescued.

The crew of the Endurance *were excited to finally see a rescue ship.*

ERNEST SHACKLETON'S ROUTE

Endurance departs

SOUTH GEORGIA

Atlantic Ocean

Pacific Ocean

ELEPHANT ISLAND

WEDDELL SEA

SOUTH AMERICA

Endurance sinks

Endurance is crushed

Endurance is trapped in ice

ANTARCTICA

—— Voyage of the Endurance ship

—— The Endurance drifts

•••••• Crew drags lifeboats across ice

•••••• Ernest sails to find help

Left for Dead at the Top of the World

It was 1996, and Beck Weathers was climbing Mount Everest. Temperatures were a bone-numbing 21 degrees below zero (-30°C). Vicious hurricane-force winds blew at 150 miles per hour (240 kph). The high altitude was making Beck go blind. He stopped climbing. He would wait at 27,000 feet (8,200 m) for his guide to pick him up on his way down the mountain.

He waited 10 hours, but his guide never returned. Beck started to make his way down with a group of climbers. A blizzard rolled in. **Visibility** was zero. The group huddled together for warmth and safety. They hit each other to stay awake. Beck lost a glove.

FUN FACT

Mount Everest is over 60 million years old. Every year, it grows about a quarter of an inch (.64cm).

The weather on Mount Everest can change very quickly.

The next morning, rescuers came. They found Beck with his jacket open. His face was covered with ice. His arms and legs were stiff. They decided he was near death. He would not make it off the mountain. They left him behind. They told his wife he had died.

Beck spent that night in the open in a blizzard with nothing covering his face or hands. He was in a **hypothermic coma** for 15 hours. In the morning, he woke up. He does not know why. He descended to a camp.

Tents can provide shelter from snow and cold winds.

Helicopter rescues on Mount Everest are rare because the mountain is so high and the air is thin.

The climbers were stunned. Beck's face was black with frostbite. His hand was frozen. They could not believe he had survived another night. They made him comfortable and left him alone in a tent. He could not move to eat or drink. The raging blizzard blocked his cries for help. But he survived.

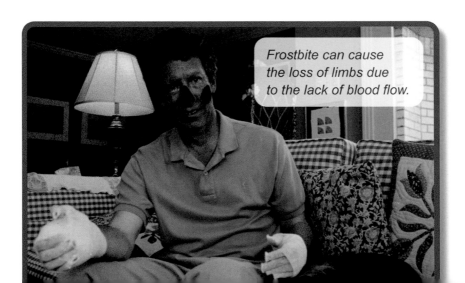

Frostbite can cause the loss of limbs due to the lack of blood flow.

The next morning, he walked on frozen feet to a lower camp. He was **evacuated** by medical helicopter. Doctors **amputated** his right hand, all his left fingers, parts of his feet, and his nose. But Beck kept his life.

YOUTH ON TOP OF THE WORLD

Mount Everest is 29,035 feet (8,850 m) high. The youngest boy to reach the summit was Jordan Romero in 2010. The youngest girl was Malavath Poorna in 2014. They were both aged 13.

THE BOOK

After reading the book, it's time to think about what you learned.
Try the following exercises to jumpstart your ideas.

THINK

DIFFERENT SOURCES. Think about the many different sources you could use to learn about blizzards. What could you find in an encyclopedia? What could you learn in other books or videos? How could each of the sources be useful in its own way?

CREATE

PRIMARY SOURCES. A primary source is an original document, photograph, or interview. Make a list of primary sources you might be able to find about blizzards. What new information might you learn from these sources?

SHARE

WHAT'S YOUR OPINION? Blizzards can be very dangerous. But some people think the challenge of climbing a giant mountain or walking across Antarctica is worth the risk. They think it should be their choice whether they go out in dangerous weather or not. Do you agree or disagree? Use evidence from the text to support your answer. Share your position and evidence with a friend. Does your friend agree with you?

GROW

REAL-LIFE RESEARCH. Think about what kinds of places you could visit to learn more about blizzards. What other topics could you explore there?

RESEARCH NINJA

Visit *www.ninjaresearcher.com/2008* to learn how
to take your research skills and book report writing to the next level!

RESEARCH  ⋯⋯⋯⋯⋯⋯⋯⋯⋯⋯⋯⋯⋯

DIGITAL LITERACY TOOLS

SEARCH LIKE A PRO
Learn how to use search engines to find useful websites.

FACT OR FAKE?
Discover how you can tell a trusted website from an untrustworthy resource.

TEXT DETECTIVE
Explore how to zero in on the information you need most.

SHOW YOUR WORK
Research responsibly—learn how to cite sources.

WRITE ⋯⋯⋯⋯⋯⋯⋯⋯⋯⋯⋯⋯⋯⋯⋯⋯⋯⋯⋯

GET TO THE POINT
Learn how to express your main ideas.

PLAN OF ATTACK
Learn prewriting exercises and create an outline.

DOWNLOADABLE REPORT FORMS

Further Resources

BOOKS

Bowman, Chris. *Survive a Blizzard*. Minneapolis, MN: Bellwether Media, 2016.

Doeden, Matt. *Surviving Antarctica: Ernest Shackleton*. Minneapolis, MN: Lerner Publications, 2019.

Herman, Gail, and Michele Amatrula. *Climbing Everest*. New York, NY: Random House Books for Young Readers, 2015.

Meister, Cari. *Blizzards*. Minneapolis, MN: Jump! 2016.

Rathburn, Betsy. *Blizzards*. Minneapolis, MN: Bellwether Media, 2020.

WEBSITES

FACTSURFER

Factsurfer.com gives you a safe, fun way to find more information.

1. Go to www.factsurfer.com.

2. Enter "Surviving a Blizzard" into the search box and click 🔍

3. Select your book cover to see a list of related websites.

Glossary

altitude: The height of something above ground level. At high altitudes, there is less oxygen, making it harder to breathe and causing dizziness and loss of energy.

amputated: Removed part of the body by surgery. Often, doctors will amputate a finger or toe when the tissue has died from frostbite.

Antarctica: The continent surrounding the South Pole. It is covered almost entirely by ice, even in the summer.

blizzard: A snowstorm with strong winds and low visibility that lasts for at least three hours. The blizzards in these stories lasted much longer.

evacuated: Took someone from a dangerous place to a safe one. When people are injured in places that are hard to reach, helicopters are used.

glaciers: Rivers of ice in the mountains made by heavily packed snow. Walking on glaciers usually requires special equipment, such as spiked boots, helmets, and ice axes.

hull: The outer body of a ship, which gives the ship its shape. When a wooden hull cracks, the ship is no longer waterproof and will most likely sink.

hypothermic coma: When a person is unconscious due to extreme cold. It is rare for a person to wake up from a hypothermic coma, especially at high altitudes.

visibility: The distance that a person can see. In a blizzard, visibility is less than 0.25 miles (0.4 km) and is often called a whiteout.

whaling station: A place where the bodies of hunted whales are brought. Often, the whale hunters live at the whaling station.

Index

PHOTO CREDITS

About the Author

Vicki C. Hayes works as a full-time writer in Seattle, where she lives with her husband, her dog, and four nearby grandchildren. She loves the snow, especially when hot chocolate is nearby.